Congratulations Victoria
and Michael! What
amazing and caring parents
you will make.

Can't wait to meet your twinsies!

Love,

Carolyn
:)

TAKE TWO!
A Celebration of Twins

FOR MICK, OF COURSE
J. P. L.

FOR CAROLINE AND AMELIA (AND BOBORDICK)
J. Y.

FOR BEN AND ANNIE
S. B.

Collection copyright © 2012 by J. Patrick Lewis and Jane Yolen
Illustrations copyright © 2012 by Sophie Blackall

"Wishing," "Waiting in the Waiting Womb," "Twins Before Birth," "Sing a Song of Sonogram," "From Here to Maternity,"
"Be Careful What You Wish For!," "First Words," "Doozy Twosies," "High Hopes," "The Song of Charlotte and Cynthia Rose (Taking a Bath),"
"What's It Like to Be a Twin?," "Big Fight: Round Two," "Fair Is Fair!," "Tree-House Treat," "Pat and Mike," "We Learned to Sing," "Harry and Hubbell,"
"At the Old Ball Game," "Sixteen Sets of Twins," "The Tweedle Twins," "Twinsburg, Ohio" copyright © 2012 by J. Patrick Lewis

"Two Dots," "Womb Mate," ". . . and After," "Be Even More Careful," "How Twins Talk," "Lullaby to the Twins," "Pairs," "Mirror Twin,"
"Even More High Hopes," "First Steps," "Very First Words," "Twinfestation," "Learning to Tie Our Shoes," "Eating with Twins," "Names,"
"We're Supposed To Be," "Big Fight: Round One," "Double Trouble," "Twindependent," "More Than One," "Two's a Crowd," "Conjoined,"
"Playing the Game" copyright © 2012 by Jane Yolen

First edition 2012

Library of Congress Cataloging-in-Publication Data

Lewis, J. Patrick.
Take two! : a celebration of twins / by J. Patrick Lewis and Jane Yolen ; illustrated by Sophie Blackall. — 1st ed.
p. cm.
ISBN 978-0-7636-3702-6
1. Twins — Juvenile poetry. I. Yolen, Jane. II. Blackall, Sophie. III. Title.
PS3562.E9465D68 2012
811'.54 — dc22 2010050564

14 15 16 17 SCP 10 9 8 7 6 5 4 3

Printed in Humen, Dongguan, China

This book was typeset in Diotima.
The illustrations were done in watercolor, pencil, and painted paper collage.

Candlewick Press
99 Dover Street
Somerville, Massachusetts 02144

visit us at www.candlewick.com

TWIN FACT *Twin* comes from the German word *twine,* which means "two together."

TAKE TWO!
A Celebration of Twins

J. Patrick Lewis *and* Jane Yolen

illustrated by Sophie Blackall

Candlewick Press

Contents

TWINS IN THE WAITING WOMB

Two Dots	8
Wishing	9
Waiting in the Waiting Womb	10
Womb Mate	11
Twins Before Birth	12
. . . and After	13
Sing a Song of Sonogram (A Sonnet)	14
From Here to Maternity	15
Be Careful What You Wish For!	16
Be Even More Careful	17

TWINFANTS

First Words	20
How Twins Talk	21
Lullaby to the Twins	22
Doozy Twosies	23
Pairs	24
Mirror Twin	25
High Hopes	26
Even More High Hopes	27
First Steps	28
Very First Words	29
The Song of Charlotte and Cynthia Rose (Taking a Bath)	30
Twinfestation	32
Learning to Tie Our Shoes	34
Eating with Twins	35
Names	36

HOW TO BE ONE

We're Supposed to Be 40

"What's It Like to Be a Twin?" 41

Big Fight: Round One 42

Big Fight: Round Two 43

Fair Is Fair! 44

Double Trouble 45

Twindependent 46

Tree-House Treat 48

More Than One 50

Two's a Crowd 51

Pat and Mike 52

We Learned to Sing 54

Harry and Hubbell 57

At the Old Ball Game 58

FAMOUS TWINS

Sixteen Sets of Twins 63

Conjoined 64

The Tweedle Twins 67

Playing the Game 68

Twinsburg, Ohio 70

Authors' Note 72

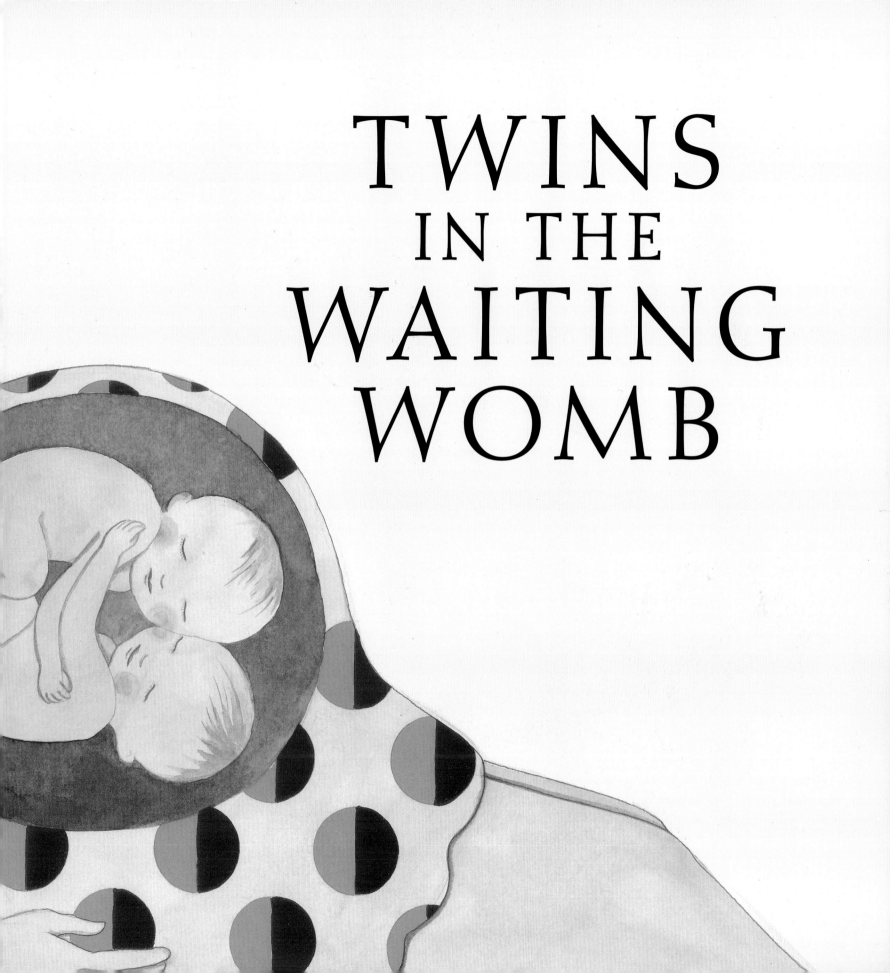

TWINS
IN THE
WAITING
WOMB

Two Dots

See that dot
Upon the screen?
That's your child.

Hope she's neither
Mad nor mean,
But rather mild.

See that other
Down below?
That's the twin.

Double mother?
Oh-oh-oh,
How to begin?

Twinside in,
Twinside out.
That's what twins
Are all about.

WISHING

Wishing for twins?
You'll be surprised
If they come out
As advertised!

TWIN FACT If a woman has already delivered one set of fraternal twins, the odds of her having a second set are one in twelve.

WAITING IN THE WAITING WOMB

Dining in the dining womb,
Getting so much stronger.

Wishing in the living womb
You could stay much longer.

Wrestling in the family womb,
You and sister linger.

Crowded in the waiting womb;
Poke her with your finger.

TWIN FACT Twins have their own constellation and zodiac sign: Gemini.

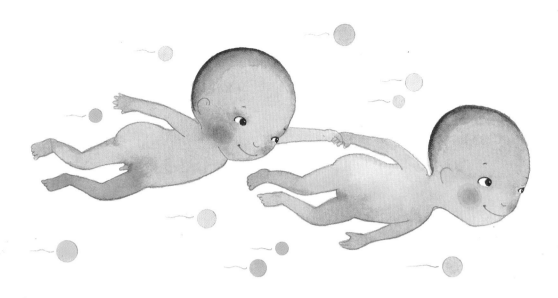

WOMB MATE

Brother, don't bother.
I'm older. I'm first.
Try to go faster.
Your bubble will burst.

We'll wait here together
Till time to appear.
Then I'll go before you,
So stay very near.

You'll always be second
And slower — you'll see.
Stop pushing, stop shoving,
And just follow me.

TWINS BEFORE BIRTH

Long after they
   burst into bloom,
They share a dark,
   rich living room

Of arms and legs,
   elbows and knees.
The room is ninety-
   eight degrees.

They may hear voices,
   homeward bound —
Is that an ultra-
   ultrasound?

But they won't know
   it's day or night
Until they see . . . .
   the light, the light!

TWIN FACT While healthy singletons usually spend 40 to 43 weeks in the womb before being born, healthy twin pregnancies generally last only 37 weeks.

. . . AND AFTER

Four hands, four knees,
Two doctors, if you please.

Four feet, four eyes,
That's a really neat surprise.

Ten toes times two,
And ten fingers — double whew!

And diapers
By the dozen dozens.
Can't wait to show you
To the cousins.

SING A SONG OF SONOGRAM

(A Sonnet)

The
twin
be-
gin-
ning!
Wow!
Sing
now —
non-
stop,
Mom,
Pop,
proud
crowd!

TWIN FACT The scientific study of twins is called *gemellology*.

From Here to Maternity

Double package deal
Ultrasound of glee
Bound to make you feel
C'est LA-LA la vie!

Be Careful What You Wish For!

You wished for a boy — two girls came out!
You got the benefit of the doubt.

* * * * * * * * * * * * * * * * * * *

You wanted two girls but got one boy:
Return the lace for the corduroy.

BE EVEN MORE CAREFUL

You wished for a singleton; now you've got two:
A single in pink and a single in blue.

You wished for a family; that's not a crime.
You wished for a family — but not at one time.

TWIN FACT Identical twins are the same sex and look exactly alike. Fraternal twins do not look alike and come in three variations: male-female (about 40 percent of all twins born), female fraternal twins (sometimes called sororal twins), and male fraternal twins.

First Words

Look at us, twin!

Hey, we're breathing!

Couple o' weeks

And we'll be teething.

Couple o' months

And no more Huggies.

Say bye-bye

To baby buggies.

Couple o' years

And no more nursery.

Happy second

Anniversary!

TWIN FACT Cryptophasia is a so-called language that some twins share when they are babies and toddlers.

How Twins Talk

Not with a *ga-ga,*
Not with a *goo,*
But with a wave
And a wink
And an *I love you.*

Lullaby to the Twins

Good night,
Good night.
The single moon
Shines down.
And soon
One sleep
You'll share.
You are
Two stars:
One dark,
One fair.
Two hearts,
Sweethearts,
And I am here.
Good night,
Good night.
Sleep tight,
Sleep tight.

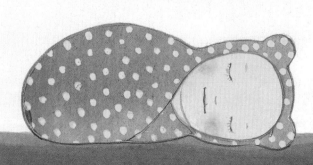

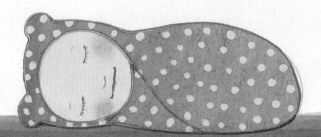

Doozy Twosies

Double the fingers,
Double the toes,
Double the diapers,
Double the nose,
Double the fannies,
Double the grins.
Double the birthdays —
Hello, TWINS!

TWIN FACT Nigeria is the nation with the highest number of multiple births.

Pairs

We are not
The only twos:
Socks come in pairs,
As well as shoes.
Eyes are double,
Hands and feet,
Legs are twosome,
Ears repeat.
All the best things
Come in two:
You with me,
And me with you.

MIRROR TWIN

I wave, you wave.

I smile, you laugh.

I wink, you blink.

You leave — I'm half.

HIGH HOPES

Imagine that! Your blessed event
Could grow up to be president!
Here comes the second girl — oh, wait.
She'll be secretary of state!

Even More High Hopes

Imagine this: your firstborn son
Will steer Mars rocket number one.
His twin will build the rocket ship
That takes him on that famous trip.

TWIN FACT The record for the lightest twins at birth is 1 pound 8 ounces for Courtney (12 ounces) and Chloe (12 ½ ounces) Smith, born in Louisiana on March 1, 2000. The record for the heaviest twins at birth is 27 pounds 12 ounces for Patricia Jane (14 pounds) and John Prosser (13 pounds 12 ounces) Haskin, born in Arkansas on February 20, 1924.

First Steps

Hold on to the table,
The back of the chair,
And I'll be there.
I'll be there.

Hold on to the banister
Of the stair,
And I'll be there.
I'll be there.

Hold on to my hand
If you dare.
We'll both be there.
We'll both be there.

VERY FIRST WORDS

Me.

You.

One.

Two.

Mine.

Twin.

I win.

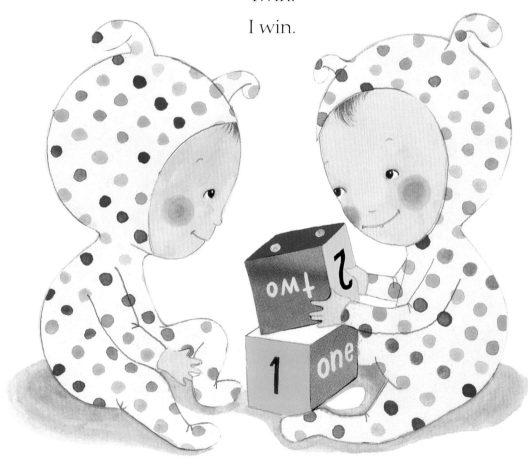

TWIN FACT There are about 125 million living multiples in the world.

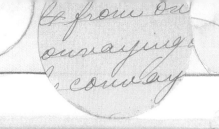

THE SONG OF CHARLOTTE AND CYNTHIA ROSE
(TAKING A BATH)

It was Saturday night; the thermometer froze.
The two of them shivered in layers of clothes.
They knew it was time for their Saturday bath,
And something inside her made Cynthia laugh.

"Listen," their mother said, "Cynthia Rose
And Charlotte, the bathwater's over your toes!"

Chorus:
Will the water be over their ankles tonight?
Will the water be up to their knees?
Will the bubbles be up to their chins tonight
In the Charlotte-and-Cynthia Seas?

They took off their scarves, their boots, and their caps.
They pulled off their red mittens, too.
Unbuttoned their coats with *snippety-snaps*.
Well, isn't that what you would do?

"Charlotte and Cynthia, hurry up, please.
The bathwater's bound to be up to your knees!"

Chorus:
Will the water be over their ankles tonight?
Will the water be up to their knees?
Will the bubbles be up to their chins tonight
In the Charlotte-and-Cynthia Seas?

They took off their shoes and their Valentine socks
(The ones with the hearts on the toes),
Took out their barrettes and then started to peel
Off several more layers of clothes.

Their mother yelled, "Girls, did you hear what I said?
The bathwater's bound to be up to your head!"

For the water rose over their ankles, all right,
And the water rose over their knees.
The bubbles rose up to their chins ALL NIGHT
In the Charlotte-and-Cynthia Seas.
One paddles, one rows with their fingers and toes
In the Charlotte-and-Cynthia Seas,
In the Charlotte-and-Cynthia Seas.

TWIN FACT   Conjoined twins occur in 1 out of 400,000 twin births.

TWINFESTATION

Some time we twincubate in Mom,
    For not quite a year;
The twindow opens up for us,
    We twinstantly appear.

Not yet quite twindividuals,
    So twinsomely we smile
With winning twincandescence,
    They let us stay awhile.

And soon, from spring to twinter,
    We've lived with them so long,
This small twinfestation
    No longer seems so wrong.

TWIN FACT The record for the tallest twins belongs to identical twins Michael and James Lanier, who are both seven foot six.

Learning to Tie Our Shoes

Every time I tie my shoe,
I think of me, I think of you,
And how the laces, side by side,
Are so much stronger when they're tied.

As one loop goes around the other,
So we twins bond — sister, brother —
Safely knotted, like a shoe,
You to me, and me to you.

Eating with Twins

Eat
    Eat
Veggies
    Meat
Bread
    Toasted
Raw
    Roasted
Eggs
    Ham
Spinach
    Spam
Crackers
    Cheese
Ice cream
    Please

TWIN FACT The first test-tube twins, Stephen and Amanda Mays, were born on June 5, 1981, in Australia.

Names

Robin and Bobby,

Jackie and Gill,

Sammy and Danni,

Wallie and Phil,

Chris and Kris,

Frankie and Coy.

Can you tell which twin's

The girl or the boy?

Mannie and Marty,

Gabby and Dan,

Jonny and Jamie,

Jackie and Fan,

Sandy and Sidney,

Leslie and Merle.

Can you tell which twin's

The boy or the girl?

TWIN FACT   Since the 1970s, the number of twin births has more than doubled.

HOW TO

We're Supposed to Be

We're supposed to be twins,
    So why are you so tall?
We're supposed to be twins,
    So why am I so small?

We're supposed to be the same,
    But you have better hair.
We're supposed to be as one.
    It really isn't fair.

"What's It Like to Be a Twin?"

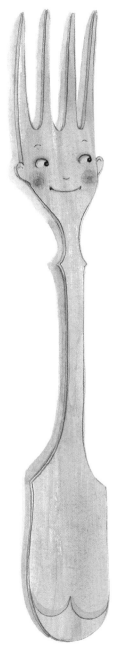

Lots and lots of people ask me,
"What's it like to be a twin?"
I tell them that your very, very,
Very next of kin
Is a hard-to-get-to tickle
Or an afternoon to snore
Or the easy teasing of a sneeze
That's pleasing. Only more.

It's sitting down to Mom's
Famous lasagna . . . only twice.
It's the way a tomcat shivers
When he's introduced to mice.
'Cause a twin's a double rainbow
Or the fork that goes with knife.
He may wear around the edges,
But he's guaranteed for life.

 TWIN FACT The Koelher twins were born in 1925 in Denton, Montana. The boy grew to eight foot two, one of the tallest men in the twentieth century. His twin sister was five foot nine.

BIG FIGHT: ROUND ONE

Amelia	Caroline
I have a twin,	A best friend, too.
We've had a fight.	What should I do?
She told a fib.	*She* told a lie.
She made me blush.	*She* made me cry.
She called me names.	*She* called me weird.
She sounded mean.	I sounded scared.
I have a twin.	What should I do?

She's who I want to be

Talking to.

Big Fight: Round Two

Caroline	Amelia
This is my doll.	Why won't she share?
She's got her own.	It's lost its hair!
She's got ice cream.	Butter pecan.
I wanted some!	It's almost gone!
She took my book.	Where's my barrette?
How should I know?	My matching set!
Here, use my clip.	Thank you, I will.

And instantly, the house is still.

FAIR IS FAIR!

What separates my twin and me,

Born twenty minutes apart,

Is that he's always first because

Of his unfair head start.

He's first to hog the bathroom

Every morning. And at dinner,

He gets the biggest helping,

Which is why I'm so much thinner.

I thought I won the marathon.

At last! Glory was mine!

Until I saw my brother — *yawning!* —

At the finish line.

But one day fate will finally turn —

I won't be sad, bereft —

He'll bite the dust, which means I must

Have twenty minutes left.

TWIN FACT The record for the longest time between a pair of twins being born is ninety-five days. Timothy Keys was born on October 15, 1993, and his twin, Celeste, on January 18, 1994.

DOUBLE TROUBLE

We both talk with our mouths full,
An ucky way to speak.
We both forget our lunches
At least two times a week.
We both are slow to get up,
We're late to go to bed;
We always find a reason
To stay awake instead.
There isn't any argument
That both have never tried,
But we protect each other
From anyone outside.

TWINDEPENDENT

I am I,
I am not you.
I live apart.
Do you live, too,
With dreams and hopes
That are your own?
Will we be two
When fully grown?

I want to be
an astronaut.
You want to live
Where it is hot.
I long for silence,
You for noise.
You play with dolls,
Planes are my toys.

I am I,
A thing apart,
Although we share
Our mother's heart,
Our father's, too,
And in our way
Our genes and all
Our DNA.

But in each
Personality
We are as one
As we can be.

TWIN FACT There is no evidence that twins can read each other's minds.

Tree-House Treat

Up in our tree house,
Spring's on parade.
We've got two cool leafy
Seats in the shade.

If you eat an apple,
I'll eat one, too —
We'll sit in the tree house
Admiring the view.

Now you go down first.
If Dad calls my name,
We'll trick him again —
Twin Switcheroo game.

Then we'll count how long
It takes him to see
That I am not you
And you are not me.

TWIN FACT Approximately 25 percent of identical twins are mirror-image twins. Their hair parts fall on opposite sides and their fingerprints are mirror images. One of them will be right-handed, the other left-handed.

MORE THAN ONE

Most times two is more than one:
More giggles, laughs,
and MUCH more fun.
But mathematics
Can prove wrong,
And two can make a day seem long
With turns to take and compromises
And never any real surprises.

Sometimes, sometimes — I think I'd like
My twin to take a long, long hike
Or ride away upon her bike
And leave me by myself a day,
Until that feeling goes away.

Two's a Crowd

If you never have a single moment
You can call your own,
Always being dubbed "the twin"
And never left alone,

You'll understand the plight I'm in,
Wishing I were one,
As if that birth date long ago
Could somehow be redone.

But when I think how awfully lonely
Singletons must be,
It's then I'm glad that I have you,
Who's such a part of me.

 TWIN FACT The record for the longest living twins is held by Eugenia (Smith) Collins and Alice (Smith) Lindsay, born in Australia on March 31, 1893. Eugenia died on October 8, 1998, at age 105, and Alice died on July 1, 2004, at 111 years old. Their combined age was 216 years and 9 months!

51

PAT AND MIKE

Now Pat and Mike
are just alike,
except that Pat
is **PASTA-FAT,**
and Mike, his twin,
is **NOODLE-THIN,**
and as for hair,
poor Pat is bare,
but Mike combs his
into a frizz.
They play hardball —
Mike is the tall
first baseman, see?
And Pat's the pee-
wee pitcher. He
throws easy strikes
to Mike, who likes
to knock the ball
over the wall,

which makes Pat grin

because his twin

pays him a dime

time after time

he serves up one

more Mike home run.

Yes, Pat is nice

but Mike is twice

as nice as Pat

is PASTA-FAT.

But Pat would love

(It's unheard of!)

to be the thin

tall NOODLE-TWIN.

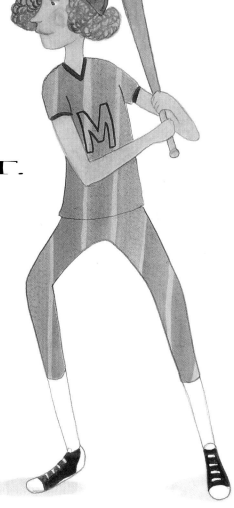

TWIN FACT Fraternal twins run only through the mother's side of the family. Identical twins just happen.

WE LEARNED TO SING

We learned the alphabet; we learned to sing
Because my twin had called it "double play."
We taught each other almost everything.

I showed her how to push me in the swing.
She's smart. She learned it quickly, the same way
We learned the alphabet and learned to sing

And entertain with puppets on a string.
Our mom and dad came for the matinee!
We taught each other almost everything.

Remember how it stung — that first bee sting?
But there she was, and it was like the day
We learned the alphabet and learned to sing.

If she was some bright bird, I was the wing.
If I was like a model, she was clay.
We taught each other almost everything.

 On average, identical twins live longer than fraternal twins, possibly due to their closeness.

From summer, autumn, winter into spring.
And after kindergarten *we* would say
The alphabet together and we'd sing.

This poem has its own familiar ring —
Two twins who stick together come what may.
We learned the alphabet and learned to sing.
We taught each other almost everything.

HARRY AND HUBBELL

Fraternal twins,
    Harry and Hubbell,
Loved to eat
    But hated to nibble,
Hated to talk
    But loved to babble,
Hated to write
    But loved to scribble,
Loved to fight
    But hated to quibble.
And that's the reason
    Why Harry and Hubbell
Were two times fun —
    And four times trouble!

 Fraternal twins are the result of two eggs fertilized at the same time. Fraternal twins share 50 percent of their DNA. They can look alike or very different. They can even be a boy-girl pair.

At the Old Ball Game

I'm your hotdog,
You're my sub,
I'm your baseball ticket stub.

You're my French fries,
I'm your shake.
You're the fun in funnel cake.

I'm your popcorn,
You're my peanuts —
Home plate ump is driving me nuts.

You're my Pepsi,
I'm your Coke.
I think we're already broke.

I'm your fastball.
You're my spitter.
Who's the designated hitter?

TWIN FACT Identical twins occur when a single egg splits. Identical twins share 100 percent of their DNA. They are always the same gender, and they look alike.

I'm your bleachers.
What the heck?
You're my right-field upper deck.

You're my super-
Duper dome!
I'm your subway — let's go home.

SIXTEEN SETS OF TWINS

You know the old woman
Who lived in a shoe?
She had so many children
She didn't know what to do.

How could the woman
Who resided in Shuya,
Have so many children?
You don't know, do ya?

TWIN FACT In the 1700s, Mrs. Feodor Vassilyev of Shuya, Russia, had sixteen sets of twins. She also gave birth to four sets of quadruplets and seven sets of triplets!

CONJOINED

Chang and Eng:

twins,

a miracle,

a curse,

joined at the chest.

Yet the rest

is history,

mystery,

and a bit of love.

They worked in a circus,

left to farm,

married sisters,

came to no harm,

fathered

twenty-one children,

singletons all.

When one slipped,

the other had to fall.

TWIN FACT Chang and Eng Bunker were born in Thailand on May 11, 1811. At age seventeen, the boys were discovered while swimming and brought to America. They toured with the P. T. Barnum circus until their retirement in 1839. On January 7, 1874, Chang, who had come down with pneumonia, passed away. His twin brother, Eng, died three hours later.

A cold winter night,
Chang died.
In a fright his brother
followed soon after.
Their lives have occasioned
much thought,
many sermons,
a few plays,
short stories,
poems —
and
laughter.

THE TWEEDLE TWINS

Tweedledum and Tweedledee
    Decided they would dance,
Especially since they wore to tea
    Those white tight-fitting pants.

No sooner had they started in,
    As Alice spun them round,
Than T. Dum bumped into his twin —
    And both fell to the ground.

They laughed till they were overcome,
    But Alice wept a tear.
Said Tweedledee and Tweedledum,
    "A sniffle? Oh, poor dear."

And so they got back up, you see,
    And took her by the hand.
All three danced to a melody
    Played by a Rubber Band.

TWIN FACT   Tweedledum and Tweedledee are nursery rhyme characters who make their most famous appearance in *Through the Looking-Glass and What Alice Found There* by Lewis Carroll, illustrated by John Tenniel, published in 1871.

Playing the Game

Baseball is a game of numbers.

Nine men to start,

the very heart

of the team.

Four balls, four bases

round which

a runner races.

Three strikes, three outs,

and many hundreds

of encouraging shouts,

like "Kill the umpire,"

"Ump is blind."

(Well, not all of them

are all that kind.)

But twos? Let's see . . .

A double can

mean victory.

Then Twins — the Minnesota sort —

and several players,

tall and short,

are twins:

Cansecos, Minors,

to name two,

O'Briens, Cliburns, Hunters —

that's a few.

Jonnards, Shannons,

and the Brothers Grimes,

who homered

quite a number of times.

Count 'em up

or count 'em out,

twins are in baseball —

without a doubt.

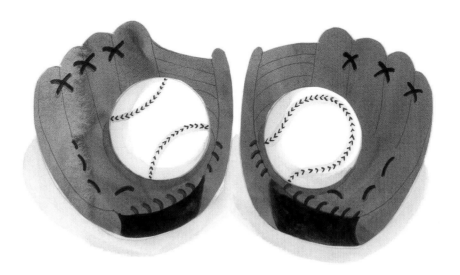

TWIN FACT   All true.

TWINSBURG, OHIO

Drop everything right where you are!
Get in the truck, the van, the car —
Here's where the double fun begins,
At Twinsburg's festival of twins.

Some twins are thick and some are thin
(Think cello next to violin).
Some are little, some are big
(Think Yorkshire next to guinea pig).

Some are white with farmers' tans,
Some are black and holding hands,
And some twins you can't tell apart
Unless you read the doctor's chart.

Some come in cummerbunds and suits,
Or Harley hogs and cowboy boots,
To sing duets and karaoke —
No one seems to care how hokey.

 In 1976, the first Twins Days Festival in Twinsburg, Ohio, attracted thirty-seven sets of twins. At the 2009 festival, 2,038 sets of twins participated.

First week in August there will be
A Twinsburg twins festivity —
Amazing! For just one low price,
You get to see one person . . .

twice!

Authors' Note

Whenever a student asks me, "What should I do if I want to be a writer?" I always say, "Get yourself a twin." That's a joke, but only by half. I am a twin, and I can tell you that being one is the best thing that's ever happened to me. Well, the third best really, after having wonderful children and grandchildren of my own, of course, and eating my mom's apple dumplings. Mick, my twin, is my first reader, my first editor, and my best friend. So any errors or weaknesses in the quality of the poems herein are half his.

— J. P. L.

I am the niece of twins (the late Eva and Sylvia Yolen), the sister-in-law of twins (Bob and Dick Stemple), and the grandmother of twins (Caroline and Amelia Stemple). In college I roomed with one twin; her sister lived in the next-door dorm. The thing to remember is that as alike as twins are, they are also distinct personalities. And they remind you about this every single day, even when they play tricks on you or have their own language or keep secrets together. So this book is not only for all the twins out there, but also for the singletons who love them and who, even after nearly fifty years, cannot always tell them apart.

— J. Y.

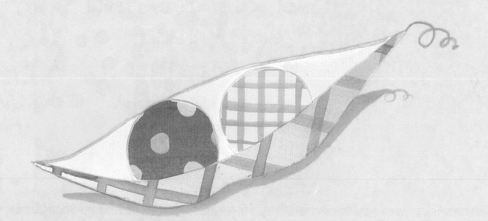